SHERLOCK H
AND THE DUKE'S SON

Are all bicycle tyres the same? How many different kinds of bicycle tyre are there? When someone cycles over soft wet ground, the tyres leave tracks on the ground – but one tyre makes a deeper track. Is it the tyre on the front wheel or the back wheel?

When the Duke's son is kidnapped from Dr Huxtable's school, it is important to know the answers to questions like these. Sherlock Holmes, and his old friend Dr Watson, spend many hours looking at the mud on Lower Gill Moor. They find the tracks of bicycle tyres, the tracks of sheep and of cows – and they also find a body. Now there are even more questions, and Dr Watson thinks it is not possible to find the answers. 'Come, come, Watson,' says Holmes. 'Every mystery has an answer.'

But even Sherlock Holmes is surprised by the answer to this mystery . . .

OXFORD BOOKWORMS LIBRARY
Crime & Mystery

Sherlock Holmes and the Duke's Son

Stage 1 (400 headwords)

Series Editor: Jennifer Bassett
Founder Editor: Tricia Hedge
Activities Editors: Jennifer Bassett and Christine Lindop

SIR ARTHUR CONAN DOYLE

Sherlock Holmes and the Duke's Son

Retold by
Jennifer Bassett

Illustrated by
Ron Tiner

OXFORD UNIVERSITY PRESS

OXFORD
UNIVERSITY PRESS

Great Clarendon Street, Oxford OX2 6DP

Oxford University Press is a department of the University of Oxford.
It furthers the University's objective of excellence in research, scholarship,
and education by publishing worldwide in

Oxford New York

Auckland Cape Town Dar es Salaam Hong Kong Karachi
Kuala Lumpur Madrid Melbourne Mexico City Nairobi
New Delhi Shanghai Taipei Toronto

With offices in

Argentina Austria Brazil Chile Czech Republic France Greece
Guatemala Hungary Italy Japan Poland Portugal Singapore
South Korea Switzerland Thailand Turkey Ukraine Vietnam

OXFORD and OXFORD ENGLISH are registered trade marks of
Oxford University Press in the UK and in certain other countries

The original version of this story was published
under the title *The Priory School*
This simplified edition © Oxford University Press 2002

Database right Oxford University Press (maker)

First published in Oxford Bookworms 1998
8 10 12 14 15 13 11 9

Any websites referred to in this publication are in the public domain and
their addresses are provided by Oxford University Press for information only.
Oxford University Press disclaims any responsibility for the content

ISBN-13: 978 0 19 422961 6
ISBN-10: 0 19 422961 0

A complete recording of this Bookworms edition of
Sherlock Holmes and the Duke's Son is available on cassette ISBN 0 19 423296 4

Printed in Hong Kong

CONTENTS

1
Sherlock Holmes has a visitor

When visitors came to see Sherlock Holmes in Baker Street, they often did surprising things. Sometimes they put their heads in their hands and cried. Sometimes they talked and talked, and couldn't stop. And sometimes they just sat there and didn't say a word. But nobody was more surprising than Dr Thorneycroft Huxtable.

He was a large man, tall, well-dressed, and important-looking. He came into the room, walked to one of the big chairs, and suddenly fell into it. He sat there, with his eyes closed, looking white and ill.

He sat there, looking white and ill.

I ran to get some water for him. Then I got my doctor's bag, and looked at him carefully.

'What is it, Watson?' said Holmes.

'He's all right, I think,' I said. 'He's just very, very tired – and probably hungry too.'

Holmes looked in the man's pockets – and found a train ticket from Mackleton, in the north of England.

'Mackleton – that's a long way,' said Holmes. 'It's not twelve o'clock yet, so he probably left home before five o'clock this morning.'

After a minute or two the man began to move, and his eyes opened. A second later he got quickly to his feet. His face was now red and unhappy.

'Mr Holmes, I am so sorry! I forgot to eat or drink anything this morning – that's why I felt ill.'

'When you feel better—' I began.

'I'm better now, thank you,' said our visitor. 'And I want very much to talk to Mr Holmes – to ask him something. Please, Mr Holmes, come back to Mackleton with me by the next train.'

'I'm sorry, that's not possible,' said Holmes. 'I'm working on two important cases – the Ferrers case and the Abergavenny case. I cannot leave London at the moment.'

'Important cases!' our visitor cried. 'But this case is very important too. You know about the kidnapping of the son of the Duke of Holdernesse three days ago . . .'

'What! The Government Minister?'

'Yes, that's him. So you didn't know . . . It's not in the newspapers yet, that's true. But Sherlock Holmes always hears news before other people, I thought.'

Holmes went to get one of his books, and began to read the page about the Duke of Holdernesse.

Holmes began to read the page about the Duke of Holdernesse.

'Holdernesse, sixth Duke. Wife: Edith, daughter of Lord Grey. One child, Lord Arthur Saltire. Houses in London, Lancashire, and Wales. Government Minister for this . . . for that . . . for the other . . . Well, well,' said Holmes. 'He's one of the greatest men in the country.'

'One of the greatest, and one of the richest,' said Dr Huxtable. 'I know, Mr Holmes, that you don't work for money, but I must tell you this. The Duke is offering five thousand pounds for news of his son, and another one thousand pounds for the name of his kidnapper.'

'That,' said Holmes, 'is a most interesting offer.' He looked at me. 'Watson, I think we are going with Dr Huxtable back to the north of England this afternoon.'

Holmes then looked at Dr Huxtable. 'Now, sir, tell me everything. What happened? When did it happen? How did it happen? And why does Dr Thorneycroft Huxtable come to ask for my help *three days later*?'

Our visitor drank some water, and began his story.

2
Dr Huxtable's story

'My school – the Priory School near Mackleton – is the best school for young boys in England,' began Dr Huxtable. 'We have the sons of Lord Soames, Lord Lever, and of many other important people. Three weeks ago Mr James Wilder, the Duke of Holdernesse's secretary, came to see me. The Duke, he said, wanted to send his son, the ten-year-old Lord Saltire, to my school.

'On the 1st of May young Lord Saltire arrived. He's a nice boy, and he soon began to like school life and to make friends. His life at home, you see, was not very happy – we all know about the Duke and his wife. The Duchess, of course, now lives in the south of France. She left the Duke about three months ago, I think. But the boy loved his mother, and was very unhappy when she left. Because of this, the Duke sent him to my school. And after two weeks with us, he was much happier.

'Then, on the night of the 13th of May, he disappeared. The way to his bedroom is through another, larger room. Two older boys sleep there. One of them never sleeps very well, and he heard and saw nothing that night. So young Arthur did not go out through that room. His window was

'There is ivy all up the wall of the house.'

open, and there is ivy all up the wall of the house. It is easy to get out of the window and down the ivy to the ground. So we think that he went out that way.

'He was in his usual school things, we think – a short black coat and dark blue trousers. We looked all through his room very carefully, but we found nothing strange, nothing unusual.

'When I learnt the news at seven o'clock on Tuesday morning, I called everybody into the big schoolroom. Then we learnt more bad news – Heidegger, the German teacher, was missing too. His room is not far from Arthur's room. Heidegger went down the ivy – we know this because we found his footprints on the ground under the window. We

6

know, too, that he was only in his coat, trousers, and shoes, because we found his shirt and his socks on the floor of his room. And he took his bicycle with him.

'Heidegger came to the school a year ago. He's a good teacher, but the boys don't like him because he isn't very friendly.

'So, Mr Holmes, we have two missing people. It's now Thursday, and there's still no news of them.'

Holmes took out a little notebook, and began to write things down.

'The boy didn't go home, of course,' he said.

'No, no. We asked at Holdernesse Hall at once,' said Dr Huxtable. 'The Duke is very afraid for his son – and I am the unhappiest man in England. Mr Holmes, you are a famous detective – please help me!'

'We found his footprints on the ground.'

7

'You make things very difficult for me,' Holmes said. 'How can I find marks in the ivy or on the ground after three days? Why didn't you come to me at once?'

'Because of the Duke,' Dr Huxtable said. 'He doesn't like people talking about his unhappy family life.'

'And what are the police doing?'

'Well, they heard about a boy and a young man at the station early on Tuesday. They looked for them, and last night they found them in Liverpool – but it was a man and his son going to visit a friend. We lost three days because of that. And last night I couldn't sleep, so I took the first train down to London this morning.'

'Well, Dr Huxtable, some more questions,' said Holmes. 'Did the boy take German lessons?'

'No.'

'So he didn't know the German teacher well, then.'

'He probably never spoke to him,' said Dr Huxtable.

'Mmm,' said Holmes. 'Does the boy have a bicycle?'

'No.'

'Was any other bicycle missing?'

'No.'

'So. Did the German teacher ride away on his bicycle in the night, with the boy on his back? I don't think so. But what happened to the bicycle? Now, what about visitors? Did the boy have any visitors the day before?'

'No.'

*'Did the German teacher ride away on his bicycle in the night,
with the boy on his back? I don't think so.'*

'Did he get any letters?'

'Yes, one letter. From his father.'

'Do you open the boys' letters, Dr Huxtable?'

'No.'

'Then how do you know that the letter was from the
father?'

'I know the Duke's handwriting. And he says that he
wrote a letter to his son.'

'Did the boy get any letters from France?'

'No, I never saw any.'

'Do you understand me, Dr Huxtable?' Holmes said. 'Did someone take the boy away, or did the boy go freely? – because he had a letter from France perhaps.'

'I don't know,' said Dr Huxtable. 'He only had letters from his father, I think.'

'Were father and son very friendly?'

'The Duke is not . . . er . . . not a very friendly man, Mr Holmes. He's not a bad father, but he is a Government Minister and has a lot of things to do.'

'So the boy felt more friendly to his mother?'

'Yes.'

'Did he say that?'

'No.'

'Did the Duke tell you, then?'

'Oh no! The Duke never talks about things like that.'

'So how do you know?'

'Mr James Wilder, the Duke's secretary, told me.'

'I see,' said Holmes. 'That last letter of the Duke's – where is it now?'

'The boy took it with him,' Dr Huxtable said. 'It's not in his room. Mr Holmes – our train leaves in half an hour.'

'Right,' said Holmes. He looked at me. 'Watson, let's get ready and go off to the north with Dr Huxtable. Perhaps we can find some answers to this mystery.'

3

Holmes and Watson go north

It was dark when we arrived at Dr Huxtable's famous school in the northern hills. We went quickly into the building out of the cold, and at once someone ran up with news for Dr Huxtable.

He looked very surprised. 'The Duke is here,' he told us. 'The Duke and Mr Wilder, his secretary, are in my office. Come and meet them.'

The Government Minister was a tall man with a long, thin face. He had red hair, and a great red beard. He looked at us, and did not smile. Next to him stood Mr Wilder, a very young man. He was small, with blue eyes, and a watchful face. He spoke first.

'The Duke is surprised, Dr Huxtable, to see Mr Sherlock Holmes here. He doesn't want people to know about this. You know that, so why didn't you speak to the Duke before you went to London?'

'But we need help,' said Dr Huxtable. 'And I—'

'Well,' said the Duke. 'Mr Holmes is here now, and perhaps he can help us.' He looked at Holmes. 'I'd like you to come and stay at Holdernesse Hall, Mr Holmes.'

'Thank you, sir,' said Holmes. 'But I would like to stay

near to the mystery, here at the school. Can I ask you one or two questions, perhaps?'

'Of course,' said the Duke.

'My questions are about the Duchess, and about money,' said Holmes.

The Government Minister was a tall man, with a great red beard.

'The Duchess knows nothing about this,' said the Duke, 'and nobody is asking me for money.'

'I see,' said Holmes. 'You wrote a letter to your son before he disappeared. When did you post it?'

'Post it?' said Mr Wilder angrily. 'The Duke does not post letters. *I* put the letter into the postbag, with all the other letters that day.'

A minute or two later the Duke and Mr Wilder left. Holmes then began at once to work on the case. We looked carefully all through the boy's bedroom, and the German teacher's room. We looked at the ivy on the wall, and we saw the footprints under the German teacher's window. But we learnt nothing new. Holmes then left the house, and only came back after eleven o'clock.

He had with him a large map. He brought it into my room and put it on the bed.

'This case is beginning to get interesting, Watson,' he said. 'Look at this map. Here is the school, you see, and here is the road. So, did the boy and the teacher go along the road when they left? No, Watson, they did not!'

'How do you know that, Holmes?' I asked.

'Because there was a policeman here – look. He was there from midnight to six in the morning, and he saw nobody on the road. I spoke to him this evening. And here at the other end, you see, is the White Horse Inn. A woman there was ill, and the family watched the road all night,

13

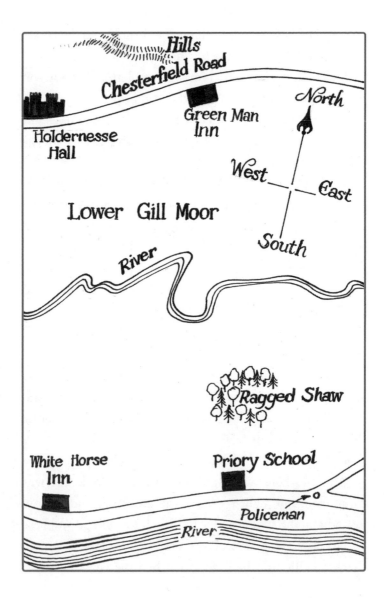

waiting for the doctor. The doctor didn't come until the morning, and the family saw nobody on the road. So the boy and the teacher did *not* go by road.'

'But, Holmes, what about the bicycle?' I asked.

'Yes, Watson, we must remember the bicycle, of course. But first, let's look to the south and the north. To the south we have a big river – no bicycles there, then. And to the north we have the trees, called Ragged Shaw, and then a great moor, the Lower Gill Moor. And here is Holdernesse Hall, sixteen kilometres from the school by road, but only nine kilometres across the moor. No other houses, until the Green Man Inn, along the Chesterfield road.'

'But the bicycle?' I said again.

'Yes, yes, Watson!' Holmes said. 'It is possible to ride a bicycle across the moor – difficult, but possible.'

Just then Dr Huxtable came quickly into the room. 'News, Mr Holmes!' he said excitedly. 'I bring news!' In his hands was a blue school hat. 'Look – this is the boy's hat. One of my gardeners found it this evening.'

'Where, man, where?' asked Holmes.

'Just north of Ragged Shaw,' said Dr Huxtable.

'Aha!' said Holmes. 'What did I tell you, Watson? Tomorrow we must walk north, across the moor.'

4
The body on the moor

Very early the next morning I opened my eyes, and saw Holmes next to my bed. He was already dressed.

'Come, Watson,' he cried. 'There is hot coffee ready for you. We leave in ten minutes.'

By six o'clock we were through Ragged Shaw, and half an hour later we were on Lower Gill Moor. Across the middle of the moor was a small river, and the ground all around it was very wet.

'We can easily see tracks in this wet ground,' said Holmes. 'Look carefully, Watson!'

We moved slowly across the moor, looking at every centimetre of mud. We found hundreds of sheep tracks, and some cow tracks – but no bicycle tracks. And then at last, we found something. Not far from the little river, right across some nice black mud, was the track of a bicycle.

'Hurrah!' I cried. 'We have it.'

But Holmes did not look happy. 'It's a bicycle, yes, but not *the* bicycle. Every bicycle has different tyres – I know forty-two different kinds of tyre. This tyre is a Dunlop, but Heidegger's bicycle had Palmer tyres. The English teacher told me that. So this is not Heidegger.'

'Is it the boy, then?' I asked.

'Probably not. The boy didn't take a bicycle with him,' said Holmes. He looked again at the track in the mud. 'This track is going away from the school.'

'Or perhaps *to* the school?' I said.

'No, no, my dear Watson. Look at the tracks of the two tyres. Are they the same?'

'Er, no,' I said. 'One tyre makes a deeper track.'

The tracks of a Dunlop tyre (left) and a Palmer tyre (right).

'And that's the back wheel,' said Holmes, 'because the rider, of course, sits over the back wheel. The deeper track is the one on top, so this bicycle went that way, across the moor away from the school. But who was the rider? Where did he come from?'

We followed the Dunlop track back, nearly to Ragged Shaw. Then we lost it, in some cow tracks. Holmes sat down and thought for some minutes.

'No,' he said, getting up. 'We must leave this question for now. Back to the mud by the river, Watson!'

Two hours later Holmes gave a happy cry. I quickly ran over to him, and looked down at a long thin track in the mud. It was the Palmer tyre.

'Here is Heidegger!' cried Holmes. 'Let's follow him, Watson.'

For a kilometre or more we followed the Palmer tyre north across the moor, losing the track, finding it again, losing it, and finding it. Suddenly, the track stopped.

'What happened here?' I said. 'Did he fall?'

Holmes looked carefully on the ground. Then he moved to some small bushes with yellow flowers on them. 'Look,' he said quietly.

On one of the yellow flowers there was something red – the dark, browny-red of blood.

'Bad!' said Holmes. 'Bad! What do I read here? Something or someone hit him. He fell, he stood up, he got onto his bicycle again, and rode away. But there is no other track. Some cow tracks here, but no footprints. We must follow the blood, Watson.'

We soon found the bicycle, and then behind a bush we saw a shoe, and found a body. There was blood on the man's head and face, and he was very, very dead. He had shoes on, but no socks, and we saw a night-shirt under his open coat. It was the German teacher.

Check Out Receipt

BPL- West End Branch Library
617-523-3957
http://www.bpl.org/branches/westend.htm

Wednesday, Sep 17 2014 4:01PM

Item: 39999052227988
Title: The scarlet letter
Material: Book
Due: 10/08/2014

Item: 39999052227723
Title: Ned Kelly : a true story
Material: Book
Due: 10/08/2014

Item: 39999052230206
Title: Sherlock Holmes and the Duke's son
Material: Book
Due: 10/08/2014

Total items: 3

Thank You!

Behind a bush, we found a body.

'Poor man,' Holmes said quietly. 'What shall we do, Watson? We can't lose any more time, but we must tell someone about this poor man.'

'Shall I run back to the school?' I said.

'No, I need you with me.' Holmes stood up and looked around. 'Look!' he said. 'There's a workman over there. He can go back to the school for us.'

I went and got the workman, and Holmes wrote a note for Dr Huxtable. The poor workman took one look at the body, and began to run quickly down the hill to Ragged Shaw.

'Now,' said Holmes, 'before we go on, let's think carefully for a minute. What do we know so far? First, the boy left freely. He was dressed, he did not leave suddenly, he wanted to go – perhaps with someone, perhaps not. But the German teacher left without his socks and without his shirt, so he left very suddenly.'

'That's right,' I said.

'And why did Heidegger go? Because, from his bedroom window, he saw the boy. Because he wanted to follow him and bring him back. So far, so good. But why doesn't Heidegger just run after the boy? A man can easily run faster than a boy – but Heidegger doesn't do this. He gets his bicycle. He knows that he *needs* his bicycle. Why?'

'Ah,' I said, 'because the boy has a bicycle.'

'Not so fast, Watson. Think about it. Heidegger dies

'Heidegger knows that he needs his bicycle. Why?'

eight kilometres from the school. So the boy is moving very fast, because it is *eight kilometres* before a man on a bicycle can get near him. And Heidegger dies because someone hits him very hard on the head. A boy can't do that, so there was *someone with the boy* – a man, let's say. But we looked very carefully at the mud all round poor Heidegger's body, Watson, and what did we find? Some cow tracks, but nothing more. No footprints from people, no bicycle tracks.'

'Holmes,' I cried. 'This is not possible.'

'Very good, Watson,' he said. 'It's *not* possible, so something is wrong with my thinking. What can it be?'

'Perhaps,' I said, 'Heidegger broke his head in a fall?'

'In mud, Watson?'

'Oh, I don't know, I just don't know.'

'Come, come, Watson,' said Holmes. 'Every mystery has an answer. But for now, the Palmer tyre can tell us nothing more, so we must go back to the Dunlop tyre.'

We found the Dunlop track again and followed it north. Here there was very little mud, and we lost the track. Across the moor we could now see Holdernesse Hall, some kilometres to our left, and in front of us we could see the Chesterfield road. We walked down to the road, and along to the Green Man Inn.

5

A visit to the Green Man

When we were near the inn, Holmes suddenly cried out. 'Aaah! My foot! I can't stand on it. Help me, Watson.'

I took his arm, and we walked slowly to the door of the inn. A man stood there, smoking, and watching us.

'How are you, Mr Reuben Hayes?' said Holmes.

'Who are you, and how do you know my name?' said the man. He looked very unfriendly.

'Because it's on the door of the inn, over your head,' said Holmes. 'But can you help me, Mr Hayes?'

'No, I can't.'

'But I need help. I can't put my foot to the ground.'

'Well, don't put it to the ground.'

Holmes smiled. 'Look,' he said. 'It's very important, and I can offer you a pound for the use of a bicycle.'

'Where do you want to go?' asked Mr Hayes.

'To Holdernesse Hall.'

'Oh, friends of the Duke, are you?' Mr Hayes laughed, looking at our muddy shoes and trousers.

Holmes laughed too. 'Well, we are bringing him news of his lost son,' he said. 'The boy is in Liverpool.'

Mr Hayes's face went white, then red. 'Oh,' he said

carefully. 'That's . . . er, that's good news. I worked for the Duke once, but he wasn't good to me. I don't like him, but I'm pleased about the boy.'

We all went into the inn. 'Now,' said Holmes,

'Oh, friends of the Duke, are you?' Mr Hayes laughed.

'something to eat first, please. Then you can bring round the bicycle.'

'I haven't got a bicycle,' said Mr Hayes.

Holmes put a pound on the table.

'I tell you, man, that I haven't got a bicycle! You can have two horses to take you to the Hall.'

He brought us something to eat, and we ate hungrily. Through the window we could see the stables at the back of the inn. Once Holmes got up and walked round the room, then stood, looking out of the window at the stables. Surprisingly, his foot was now very much better.

Suddenly he laughed, and looked at me. 'I've got it!' he cried. 'Yes, of course that's it. Watson, did you see any cow tracks today?'

'Yes,' I said. 'Lots of them. Everywhere.'

'And how many cows did you see on the moor?'

'I don't remember any,' I said.

'Isn't that strange, Watson? Lots of cow tracks, but no cows? And do you remember those tracks, Watson?' He took out his notebook. 'There were tracks like this:

$$: \; : \; : \; : \; : \; : \; : \; : \; : \; :$$

and sometimes like this:

$$: \, . \, : \, . \, : \, . \, : \, . \, : \, . \, : \, .$$

and sometimes like this:

$$. \quad . \quad . \quad . \quad . \quad . \quad . .$$

Do you remember that, Watson?'

'No, I don't,' I said. 'What does it mean, Holmes?'

'It means that it's a very strange cow, Watson! Cows don't move like that. Now, let's go quietly out and have a look round these stables.'

Holmes looked carefully at one of the horse's feet.

There were two tired-looking horses in the stables. Holmes looked carefully at one of the horse's feet, and laughed. 'Look, Watson. Old shoes, but new nails. Oh, this case gets more interesting every minute.'

I began to ask Holmes a question, but suddenly we heard someone behind us, and there was Mr Reuben Hayes. His face was red and angry.

'What are you doing in my stables?' he cried.

'We're just looking at your horses, Mr Hayes,' said Holmes, smiling. 'Why? Are you afraid of something?'

The man opened his mouth, then closed it quickly. His face was still red and angry. Holmes did not give him time to speak.

'I think your horses are tired, Mr Hayes. We can walk to the Hall. It's not far.'

'Three kilometres, by the road,' Mr Hayes said. His eyes still watched us angrily.

It was nearly dark when we left. We walked along the road for about a hundred metres. Then Holmes took my arm. 'Quick, Watson! Off the road and up the hill. Then we can come down the hill at the back of the inn.'

We ran up the hill. 'This man Hayes,' I said. 'He knows all about the kidnapping. Is that right, Holmes?'

'Of course it is,' he said. 'We can learn a lot more from Mr Hayes. Ah! Who's this? Watson, get down!'

There was a bicycle on the road. It came past us very

*Then a man on a horse rode quickly out of the stables
and disappeared down the road.*

quickly, and we saw the rider – Mr James Wilder, the Duke's secretary. His face was white and afraid.

'Quick, Watson!' said Holmes. 'We must watch him.'

We ran down the hill, and stopped when we could see the back door of the inn. Wilder's bicycle was by the wall near the door. For five minutes, nothing happened; then a man on a horse rode quickly out of the stables and disappeared down the road.

'What do you think of that, Watson?' said Holmes.

'Somebody's running away.'

'Yes. But not James Wilder, because there he is at the door.'

We could see Wilder in the light from the door. He stood there, looking out, and ten minutes later another man came down the road and went into the inn. Then a light came on in a room upstairs.

'Come, Watson. We must get nearer,' Holmes said.

We went down the hill and walked very quietly to the back door of the inn. The bicycle was still by the wall. Holmes looked at the wheel, and laughed quietly.

'A Dunlop tyre, Watson! Now, I must look through that upstairs window, so I need your back, Watson.'

Holmes stood on my back, but only for a second, and then he was down again. 'Come, my friend,' he said. 'It's a long walk to the school, so let's start at once. I can give you all the answers to this mystery tomorrow.'

It was a long, cold, muddy walk back to the school. I went to bed at once, but Holmes went out again, to Mackleton, I think. I was very tired, and slept all night like a dead man.

It was a long, cold, muddy walk back to the school.

6
Sherlock Holmes talks to the Duke

At eleven o'clock the next morning Holmes and I were in the Duke's office at Holdernesse Hall. Mr Wilder came to speak to us.

'The Duke can see no one today,' he said to Holmes.

Holmes looked at him coldly. 'The Duke can see me,' he said. 'Please tell him that I am here.'

After half an hour the Duke of Holdernesse came into the room. He looked older – tired and ill.

'Well, Mr Holmes?' he said.

Holmes looked at James Wilder. 'I can speak more freely without your secretary here, sir.'

'Very well,' said the Duke tiredly. 'Please, James . . .'

James Wilder gave Holmes an angry look, but he went out of the room and shut the door.

Holmes looked at the Duke. 'You are offering, I hear, five thousand pounds for news of your son.'

'True.'

'And another thousand pounds for the name of the kidnapper.'

'True.'

My friend smiled. 'I see your cheque book on the table,

sir. I would like to have your cheque for six thousand pounds.'

'Mr Sherlock Holmes,' the Duke said angrily, 'what is this about? Do you have news of my son, or not?'

'Oh, yes,' said Holmes.

The Duke's eyes never left Holmes's face. 'Where is my son?' he said quietly.

'He is – or was last night – at the Green Man Inn, three kilometres along the road to Chesterfield.'

The Duke fell back in his chair.

'And the name of the kidnapper?'

Sherlock Holmes's answer was a very surprising one. '*You*,' he said. 'And now, sir, your cheque, please.'

The Duke stood up, his face white and angry. Then he sat down again, and put his face in his hands. It was some minutes before he spoke.

'How much do you know?' he asked.

'I saw you with him last night,' said Holmes.

'And how many people know about this?'

'Only I and my friend here, Dr Watson.'

The Duke took out a pen, opened his cheque book, and began to write. 'When I made this offer, I didn't know . . .' He stopped, then began again. 'Are you and your friend going to talk about this, Mr Holmes?'

'I don't understand you, sir,' said Holmes.

'I mean . . . Nobody needs to know about this – this little

The Duke took out a pen and opened his cheque book.

family mystery. Just you and your friend Watson. Look, here is my cheque for twelve thousand pounds.'

Holmes gave him a cold little smile. 'I'm sorry, sir. There is a dead man in this case. You remember?'

'But that wasn't James!' cried the Duke. 'He knew nothing about it. He was very, very unhappy when he heard about the – the killing.'

'Murder,' said Holmes.

'But James wasn't there! And when he heard about it, he came to me at once, and told me everything. Oh, Mr Holmes, you must help him – you must! He is not the murderer! The murderer ran away last night.'

Holmes smiled again. 'I have a little more news for you,

sir. The police met Mr Reuben Hayes last night at Chesterfield station. Mr Hayes is not running anywhere for a very long time.'

The Duke looked at Holmes with an open mouth. 'You – you know everything!' he said. 'But I am pleased to hear about Hayes – he was always a bad man. And that news can only help James.'

'James? Your secretary?' said Holmes.

'No, sir. My son. James Wilder is my son.'

'*The police met Mr Reuben Hayes at Chesterfield station.*'

7
The Duke's son

When the Duke said this, I was very surprised, but Holmes was surprised too.

'This is news to me,' he said. 'Can you tell me more?'

The Duke stood up, and walked round the room for a minute. 'I must tell you everything,' he said. 'I didn't want to talk about it, but I must. I see that now.'

He sat down again, and began his story. 'When I was a young man, Mr Holmes, I was in love – oh, so much in love. It only happens to you once, and this woman was the love of my life. I wanted her to be my wife – but she died. She left me this one child, and I loved him because of her. When I look in his face, I see her, and remember her, and can't stop loving her. I must have the boy near me because of this. But a government minister cannot tell the world about a love-child like this. So, to the world, James is my young secretary, not my son.

'He knows that I am his father. He hates the Duchess, because she is not his mother. And he hates my younger son, Arthur, because Arthur has everything. Arthur has a name, a famous father, houses, money, everything. James has nothing. Well, he has some money, of course, but he is just Mr James Wilder, and he wants to be the Duke of Holdernesse one day. That's not possible, of course, but James can't understand that. And so, you see, I was afraid for Arthur, and that's why I sent him to Dr Huxtable's school.

'And what does James do next? He kidnaps my poor Arthur. It changes nothing, but James can't see that. He wants me to say, "Yes, James, now you can be my first son; you can have everything. Arthur can be the number two son." But I can't do that, of course I can't.

'James knew this man Hayes, you see, because Hayes worked for me once. James asked for Hayes's help, and the man was happy to do it. You remember my letter to Arthur on that last day? Well, James opened the letter and put in a note from him. That evening he cycled across the moor and met Arthur in Ragged Shaw. He talked about the Duchess, Arthur's mother. "She wants to see you," he told Arthur. "She's waiting on the moor. Come back at midnight, and a man with a horse can take you to her." Of course, poor Arthur wanted to see his mother, so he came. Hayes was there with two horses, and they rode across the moor. But the German teacher followed them, and Hayes killed him. Hayes then took Arthur to the Green Man.

'Well, Mr Holmes, I knew nothing about any of this – until the murder. James is a bad boy, but he does not murder people. When he heard the news, he came to me at once, crying. What could I do? I didn't want the world to know about this. So James went down to the Green Man. He told Hayes to run away, because everybody knew about the murder now – and knew the murderer's name too.

'That evening James met Arthur in Ragged Shaw.'

Hayes left at once. Later, I went down and saw Arthur. I left him there with Mrs Hayes because I couldn't say anything to the police just then.

'So, Mr Holmes, now you know everything.'

'Mmm,' said Holmes. 'You help a murderer, you say nothing to the police, you leave your young son in a dirty inn . . . and you ask for my help.'

People never spoke to the Duke of Holdernesse like this usually. His face was red, but he said nothing.

'First,' said Holmes, 'we must bring Arthur home.'

'Yes,' the Duke said quietly.

Holmes quickly wrote a note and took it out of the room. A minute later, he was back. 'Now, what are you going to do about Mr James Wilder?' he said.

'I understand you, Mr Holmes,' said the Duke. 'James is leaving me and going to Australia next week.'

'Good,' said Holmes. 'And the Duchess? Perhaps without James in the house, you and she . . .'

'Yes. I wrote to the Duchess this morning.'

Holmes stood up. 'Well,' he said, 'Watson and I can go home now, I think. There is just one other small thing . . . This man Hayes took two horses across the moor, but the horses' feet made the tracks of a cow in the mud. How was this possible?'

The Duke looked surprised and thought for a minute. Then he went away and came back two minutes later with a glass box in his hands. In the box were some horse-shoes.

'We found these shoes under the ground in the garden,' the Duke said. 'They are about five hundred years old, we think. The Holdernesse family has a long and interesting past.'

Holmes opened the box and took out one shoe. It was a shoe for a horse's foot, but it looked like a cloven cow's foot. Holmes wet his finger and ran it round the bottom of the shoe. A little mud came off on his finger.

'Thank you,' said Holmes. He put the horse-shoe back

It was a shoe for a horse's foot, but it looked like a cloven cow's foot.

in its box. 'That shoe is the second most interesting thing in the north of England,' he said.

'And the first?' asked the Duke.

Holmes took the cheque for twelve thousand pounds from the table, and slowly put it into his notebook. 'I am a poor man,' he said. He looked lovingly at the notebook, then put it carefully in his pocket.

'I am a poor man,' said Holmes.

GLOSSARY

beard the hair on a man's face

blood the red liquid inside your body

bush a plant like a small tree

case a problem that the police must find an answer to

cheque a piece of paper from a bank; you write on it and use it to pay money to people

cloven (of the foot of a cow, sheep, etc.) divided in two parts

cow a large animal that gives milk

deep something that is deep goes down a long way

disappear to go away so people cannot see you

Duke/Duchess a man/woman who has a special title (Miss, Dr, King, etc. are titles)

fall (past tense **fell**) to go down quickly; to drop

floor in a room, the floor is under your feet

follow to go or come after somebody or something

footprint a mark that a foot or shoe makes on the ground

Government Minister an important person in a government (the group of people that control a country)

great very important; very big

ground the sky is over your head, the ground is under your feet

hate *(v)* opposite of 'to love'

horse a big animal that can carry people on its back

inn a building where you can buy food and drink

ivy a plant with dark green leaves, that climbs up walls and trees

kidnap to take someone away and hide them, usually to get money from their family or friends

kidnapper a person who kidnaps somebody

Lord a man (or boy) with a special title

map a drawing of a place, showing roads, rivers, mountains, etc.

missing lost, or not in the usual place

moor wild land on hills, with not many trees

mud soft wet earth

murder *(v & n)* to kill somebody

mystery something strange that you cannot understand or explain

nail a small thin piece of metal, used to fix things together

newspaper you read a newspaper every day to find out what is happening in the world

offer *(v & n)* to say someone can have something

police a group of people whose job is to catch criminals

possible if something is possible, it can happen

probably almost certainly (you feel sure something is going to happen)

ride (past tense **rode**) to sit on a horse or bicycle and make it move

secretary somebody who writes letters and does other office work for another person

sheep a farm animal, used for its wool and for meat

sock you wear socks on your feet, inside your shoes

stable a building that horses live in

strange very unusual or surprising

surprised you feel surprised when something very new or strange happens

surprising if something is surprising, you feel surprised

tracks a line of marks that an animal, a person, a bicycle, etc. makes on the ground

tyre a circle of rubber round the outside of a wheel

wall a side of a building or a room

wet not dry; with water in it

Sherlock Holmes
and the Duke's Son

ACTIVITIES

Before Reading

1 Read the back cover of the book, and the introduction on the first page. How much do you know now about the story? Tick one box for each sentence.

	YES	NO
1 Someone kidnaps the Duke of Holdernesse.	☐	☐
2 The Duke's son goes to Dr Huxtable's school.	☐	☐
3 Dr Huxtable asks Sherlock Holmes for help.	☐	☐
4 Holmes and Watson look for tracks in mud.	☐	☐
5 Holmes and Watson find many bicycle tyres on the moor.	☐	☐
6 All bicycle tyres are the same.	☐	☐
7 Holmes and Watson find a dead body.	☐	☐

2 Some of these things and people are important for finding the answer to the mystery. Can you guess which? Tick eight of these fifteen boxes.

☐ cow tracks	☐ mud	☐ the English teacher
☐ sheep tracks	☐ water	☐ the German teacher
☐ bicycles	☐ a hat	☐ the Duke's secretary
☐ horses	☐ a coat	☐ the Duke's wife
☐ trains	☐ shoes	☐ the Duke's daughter

While Reading

Read Chapters 1, 2 and 3. How much do we know now about the mystery? Which of these sentences are true, and which are possibly true (but we don't really know yet)?

1 The Duke's son, Arthur, disappeared on 13th May.
2 Someone kidnapped Arthur.
3 The German teacher disappeared the same night.
4 Heidegger took his bicycle with him.
5 Arthur left the school with Heidegger.
6 Arthur ran away because of his father's letter.
7 Arthur liked his mother better than his father.
8 The Duchess knew nothing about Arthur disappearing.
9 James Wilder posted the Duke's letter to Arthur.
10 Arthur and Heidegger did not leave by road.
11 Heidegger rode his bicycle across the moor.
12 Arthur went north, through Ragged Shaw, to the moor.

Before you read Chapter 4 (*The body on the moor*), can you guess what happens? Choose one answer each time.

1 Holmes and Watson find a body. Who is it?
   a) Arthur   b) Heidegger   c) another person
2 What do they find near the body?
   a) the Duke's letter   b) footprints   c) a bicycle

Read Chapters 4 and 5, and read these questions. We know some of the answers now, but not all of them. Answer the questions when you can, and write 'Don't know yet' for the others.

1 Who rode a bicycle with Palmer tyres?
2 Whose body did Holmes and Watson find?
3 How did this person die?
4 Who killed him?
5 Did Heidegger leave the school suddenly? How do we know?
6 How did Arthur travel across the moor?
7 Why did Holmes ask Reuben Hayes for a bicycle?
8 What was interesting about the cow tracks?
9 What did Reuben Hayes know about the kidnapping?
10 Who rode the bicycle with Dunlop tyres?
11 Why did Holmes go out again that night, to Mackleton?

Before you read Chapter 6, can you guess the answers to these questions? Choose answers from these names.

James Wilder / Dr Huxtable / the Duke / Reuben Hayes / the English teacher / Arthur

1 Who rode away from the Green Man inn on a horse?
2 Who came down the road and went into the inn?
3 Who did Sherlock Holmes see in the upstairs room of the inn?

Read Chapter 6, and answer these questions.

1 Who did Holmes say was the kidnapper?
2 Why do you think the Duke wrote a cheque for twelve thousand pounds, not six thousand pounds?
3 Who killed Heidegger?
4 Why did the police go to Chesterfield station?
5 What surprising thing do we learn about the Duke's family?

How does the story end? Before you read Chapter 7, look at these sentences. Can you guess how many are true? Choose as many as you like.

1 Arthur's mother was not James Wilder's mother.
2 The Duke kidnapped Arthur because he did not want the Duchess to take Arthur to France.
3 The Duchess kidnapped Arthur.
4 James Wilder hates his brother.
5 Arthur goes to live in France with his mother.
6 James Wilder goes to Australia.
7 James Wilder goes to prison.
8 The Duke loses his job as a government minister.
9 The Duke explains the mystery of the cow tracks.
10 Sherlock Holmes tells the police everything.
11 Sherlock Holmes gives the cheque for twelve thousand pounds back to the Duke.

After Reading

1 **Match the names with the sentences. Then use the sentences to write about the people. Use pronouns (*he, him*) and linking words (*and, but, so, because*) where possible.**

the Duke / Arthur / James Wilder / Reuben Hayes / Heidegger

Example: *Arthur was the Duke's younger son.* **He** *met Reuben Hayes in Ragged Shaw one night* **because he** . . .

1 <u>Arthur</u> was the Duke's younger son.
2 _____ taught German at Dr Huxtable's school.
3 _____ did not want people to know about his love-child.
4 _____ worked for the Duke once.
5 _____ knew that the Duke was his father.
6 _____ saw Arthur from his bedroom window.
7 _____ hated Arthur.
8 <u>Arthur</u> met Reuben Hayes in Ragged Shaw one night.
9 _____ did not like the Duke.
10 _____ wanted to have James near him.
11 _____ was happy to help with the kidnapping.
12 _____ wanted to see his mother.
13 _____ wanted to be the Duke's number one son.
14 _____ gave James a job as his secretary.
15 _____ got his bicycle and followed Arthur to the moor.

2 Here is a new illustration for the story. Find the best place in the story to put the picture, and answer these questions.

The picture goes on page _____.

1 Where are Holmes and Watson?
2 Why is Holmes standing on Watson's back?
3 Who are the three people in the upstairs room?

Now write a caption for the illustration.

Caption: _____

3 **What did James Wilder say to the Duke? Put their conversation in the right order, and write in the speakers' names. James Wilder speaks first (number 7).**

1 _____ 'Yes, I do. It – it was Reuben Hayes.'

2 _____ 'But you can't be my first son – you know that.'

3 _____ 'No, it wasn't. Someone . . . killed him.'

4 _____ 'Helped you kidnap Arthur? You mean, *you* kidnapped Arthur? Why? In God's name, *why*?'

5 _____ 'But why not? Why can't I have your name and call you "father"?'

6 _____ 'Dead! But what happened? Was it an accident?'

7 _____ 'Oh sir, they found the German teacher on the moor – he's dead! What shall I do? Please help me!'

8 _____ 'How do you know it was Hayes?'

9 _____ 'Because I hate him. I'm your first son, not him!'

10 _____ 'Because I wasn't married to your mother! This is the end, James. You must go away – for ever.'

11 _____ 'Because Hayes helped me kidnap Arthur. The German teacher saw them, and Hayes killed him.'

12 _____ 'Who? Do you know, James?'

4 **What does Holmes tell Dr Huxtable? Use these words (one for each gap) to complete the passage.**

Australia, cheque, gave, happy, help, home, horse-shoes, kidnapped, kill, learnt, money, murdered, police, secretary, told, unhappy

'Well, Dr Huxtable, the story has a _____ ending for Arthur. He is now back at _____, the _____ have Reuben Hayes, and the Duke's _____ is going to _____. James Wilder wanted _____ from the Duke, you see, so he _____ Arthur, with the _____ of Reuben Hayes. But Wilder did not want to _____ anyone, and when Hayes _____ poor Heidegger, Wilder was very _____ and _____ the Duke everything. So there we are. I _____ something very interesting about _____, and the Duke _____ me a large _____.'

What did Holmes *not* tell Dr Huxtable? Why not? And what did Holmes say that was not really true?

5 **Why did Sherlock Holmes take the Duke's cheque? How many of these answers do you think are good ones? Choose as many as you like.**

1 Sherlock Holmes liked money and wanted more of it.
2 He worked hard to find the answer to the mystery, so it was right for him to take the money.
3 He wanted Dr Watson to have half the money.
4 He didn't want the money, but he wanted to punish the Duke in some way.
5 He wanted to give the money to Heidegger's family in Germany.
6 He wanted to take the cheque, and then give it back to the Duke later, when James Wilder was in Australia.

ABOUT THE AUTHOR

Sir Arthur Conan Doyle (1859–1930) was born in Edinburgh, Scotland. He studied medicine and worked as a doctor for eight years. But he needed more money, so he began writing short stories for weekly magazines.

In his first novel, *A Study in Scarlet* (1887), Sherlock Holmes appeared for the first time – a strange, but very clever detective, who smokes a pipe, plays the violin, and lives at 221B Baker Street in London. He can find the answer to almost any problem, and likes to explain how easy it is to his slow-thinking friend, Dr Watson ('Elementary, my dear Watson!'). Sherlock Holmes appeared again in *The Sign of Four* (1890), and short stories about him, in the *Strand* magazine, were very popular.

Conan Doyle himself was more interested in writing novels about history, like *The White Company* (1891), and he became bored with Sherlock Holmes. So, in the short story called *The Final Problem* (1893), he 'killed' him, and Holmes and his famous enemy, Moriarty, fell to their deaths in the Reichenbach falls. But Conan Doyle's readers were very unhappy about this because they wanted more stories about Holmes, so Conan Doyle had to bring Holmes back to life, in *The Hound of the Baskervilles* (1902) – perhaps the most famous of all the Sherlock Holmes stories.

There are more than fifty short stories about Sherlock Holmes. You can read them in almost any language, and there are many plays and films about the great detective.

ABOUT BOOKWORMS

OXFORD BOOKWORMS LIBRARY
Classics • True Stories • Fantasy & Horror • Human Interest
Crime & Mystery • Thriller & Adventure

The OXFORD BOOKWORMS LIBRARY offers a wide range of original and adapted stories, both classic and modern, which take learners from elementary to advanced level through six carefully graded language stages:

Stage 1 (400 headwords)	**Stage 4** (1400 headwords)
Stage 2 (700 headwords)	**Stage 5** (1800 headwords)
Stage 3 (1000 headwords)	**Stage 6** (2500 headwords)

More than fifty titles are also available on cassette, and there are many titles at Stages 1 to 4 which are specially recommended for younger learners. In addition to the introductions and activities in each Bookworm, resource material includes photocopiable test worksheets and Teacher's Handbooks, which contain advice on running a class library and using cassettes, and the answers for the activities in the books.

Several other series are linked to the OXFORD BOOKWORMS LIBRARY. They range from highly illustrated readers for young learners, to playscripts, non-fiction readers, and unsimplified texts for advanced learners.

Oxford Bookworms Starters	*Oxford Bookworms Factfiles*
Oxford Bookworms Playscripts	*Oxford Bookworms Collection*

Details of these series and a full list of all titles in the OXFORD BOOKWORMS LIBRARY can be found in the *Oxford English* catalogues. A selection of titles from the OXFORD BOOKWORMS LIBRARY can be found on the next pages.

Love or Money?

ROWENA AKINYEMI

It is Molly Clarkson's fiftieth birthday. She is having a party. She is rich, but she is having a small party – only four people. Four people, however, who all need the same thing: they need her money. She will not give them the money, so they are waiting for her to die. And there are other people who are also waiting for her to die.

But one person can't wait. And so, on her fiftieth birthday, Molly Clarkson is going to die.

Goodbye, Mr Hollywood

JOHN ESCOTT

Nick Lortz is sitting outside a café in Whistler, a village in the Canadian mountains, when a stranger comes and sits next to him. She's young, pretty, and has a beautiful smile. Nick is happy to sit and talk with her.

But why does she call Nick 'Mr Hollywood'? Why does she give him a big kiss when she leaves? And who is the man at the next table – the man with short white hair?

Nick learns the answers to these questions three long days later – in a police station on Vancouver Island.

The Omega Files

JENNIFER BASSETT

In EDI (the European Department of Intelligence in Brussels) there are some very secret files – the Omega Files. There are strange, surprising, and sometimes horrible stories in these files, but not many people know about them. You never read about them in the newspapers.

Hawker and Jude know all about the Omega Files, because they work for EDI. They think fast, they move fast, and they learn some very strange things. They go all over the world, asking difficult questions in dangerous places, but they don't always find the answers . . .

White Death

TIM VICARY

Sarah Harland is nineteen, and she is in prison. At the airport, they find heroin in her bag. So, now she is waiting to go to court. If the court decides that it was her heroin, then she must die.

She says she did not do it. But if she did not, who did? Only two people can help Sarah: her mother, and an old boyfriend who does not love her now. Can they work together? Can they find the real criminal before it is too late?

The Lottery Winner

ROSEMARY BORDER

Everybody wants to win the lottery. A million pounds, perhaps five million, even ten million. How wonderful! Emma Carter buys a ticket for the lottery every week, and puts the ticket carefully in her bag. She is seventy-three years old and does not have much money. She would like to visit her son in Australia, but aeroplane tickets are very expensive.

Jason Williams buys lottery tickets every week too. But he is not a very nice young man. He steals things. He hits old ladies in the street, snatches their bags and runs away . . .

The Murders in the Rue Morgue

EDGAR ALLAN POE

Retold by Jennifer Bassett

The room was on the fourth floor, and the door was locked – with the key on the inside. The windows were closed and fastened – on the inside. The chimney was too narrow for a cat to get through. So how did the murderer escape? And whose were the two angry voices heard by the neighbours as they ran up the stairs? Nobody in Paris could find any answers to this mystery.

Except Auguste Dupin, who could see further and think more clearly than other people. The answers to the mystery were all there, but only a clever man could see them.